Breaking Rank

A citizens' review of Canada's military spending

by Steven Staples

Director,
Project on the Corporate-Security State
Polaris Institute, Ottawa

Steven Staples

Steven Staples is the Director of the Polaris Institute's Project on the Corporate-Security State. He has been a writer, researcher and commentator on military and globalization issues since 1992. The Polaris Institute is a public interest research organization based in Ottawa.

Published in December 2002 by The Polaris Institute
312 Cooper Street
Ottawa, Ontario Canada K2P 0G7
Tel (613) 237-1717 Fax (613) 237-3359
polarisinstitute@on.aibn.com
http://www.polarisinstitute.org
Printed and bound in Canada

Cover and text design by Peter Coombes
Proofreading by Katharine Odgers

National Library of Canada Cataloguing in Publication

Staples, Steven
Breaking rank : a citizens' review of Canada's military
spending / written by Steven Staples.

ISBN 0-9732206-0-0

1. Canada—Military policy—Economic aspects. 2. Canada—Defenses—
Economic aspects. 3. Canada—Military relations—United States.
4. United States—Military relations—Canada. 5. Canada. Armed Forces—
Appropriations and expenditures. I. Polaris Institute II. Title.

FC603.S68 2002   355'.033071   C2002-905913-5
                        F1028.S68 2002

Note on methodology

Breaking Rank uses actual spending figures for the Department of National Defence to describe Canada's military spending. These figures provide the most accurate measurement of gross military spending (see Box 1 on page 9). In most cases, figures have been adjusted to 2001 dollars.

For the current fiscal year, the report uses estimates of gross spending by DND for 2002-2003, with the exception of Figure 1 on page 8, where the 2002-2003 fiscal year includes expected cost overruns and a war in Iraq, and Table 3 on page 10 where budgeted amounts in U.S. dollars are used for comparison purposes only.

Discussing military spending can be confusing because there are three common ways to measure and compare military spending. The most common method of comparing nations' military spending is as a percentage of a nation's Gross Domestic Product (GDP). The other methods are by measuring the number of dollars spent on the military, and by the number of dollars spent divided by the total population (per capita).

Each method of measuring and comparing military spending can generate very different rankings of countries from the highest spender to the lowest spender (see Table 3 on page 10). The method used is premised upon how the amount of a nation's military spending is properly determined.

Breaking Rank uses the number of dollars spent to measure and compare levels of military spending, because these figures should reflect the minimum amount necessary to meet a nation's legitimate defensive needs as determined by external threats, vulnerabilities, etc. This method conforms to the goal expressed in Article 26 of the United Nations' Charter: "To promote the establishment and maintenance of international peace and security with the least diversion for armaments of the world's human and economic resources..."

Contents

Acknowledgements

I wish to acknowledge the assistance of Tony Clarke, Director of the Polaris Institute, Mike Wallace of the Liu Centre for the Study of Global Issues and Professor of Political Science at the University of British Columbia, Mel Watkins, Professor Emeritus of Economics and Political Science at the University of Toronto and immediate past president of Science for Peace, and Bill Robinson, former Program Associate of Project Ploughshares, who acted as reviewers for this report and provided valuable suggestions and comments. My special thanks to Bill, who also assisted greatly in the statistical research for the report.

I am especially grateful to Peter Coombes and Katharine Odgers of the Public Education for Peace Society, Jillian Skeet of the Women's International League for Peace and Freedom, Marc Lee of the Canadian Centre for Policy Alternatives, Carolyn Basset of the Canadian Peace Alliance, Cec Muldrew of Veterans Against Nuclear Arms, Jan Slakov of the Voice of Women for Peace, David Langille of the Centre for Social Justice, and Alice Slater of the Global Resources Action Center for the Environment, who provided additional comments and support.

Finally, I wish to acknowledge the financial support of the Grace Public Fund, The Canadian Peace Alliance, the Voice of Women for Peace, the Women's International League for Peace and Freedom, Veterans Against Nuclear Arms, the Public Education for Peace Society, and the Centre for Social Justice, which made this report possible.

Preface

As the sound of war drums intensifies around us, it is becoming increasingly clear that we are at the dawn of a new era. Not only are we witnessing the resurgence of the American Empire through President Bush's doctrine on the supreme role of the U.S. as the dominant military power and policeman of the world, but since September 11th we have also seen signs of Fortress North America emerging as the U.S. begins to build a common security regime around this continent through its new homeland security agency.

So, what role is Canada expected to play in this new era of global and continental militarization? What is the current status of military spending in Canada? What forces and pressures are at work to massively increase Canada's military spending? What corporations stand to gain by increased military spending in this country? What impact will this have on social priorities such as health care and other public services? What does this say about Canada's role as a military and economic satellite of the U.S.?

These are the types of questions that *Breaking Rank* attempts to address. It is designed to provide Canadians with the kind of background information needed to make important decisions about the future of military spending by Canada in what is becoming a global war economy. This report also comes at a time when Canadians are pondering the issues arising from deeper integration with the United States — issues which, in large part, are being driven by military as well as economic dynamics.

We hope that this review of Canada's military spending will contribute to this crucial public debate that is about to unfold.

Tony Clarke, Director
Polaris Institute
Ottawa.

Summary

Main findings:

- There should be no increase in Canada's military spending. More military spending will not increase Canadians' security, and the Department of National Defence can spend defence dollars more wisely.

- Canada's military spending is already very high by international comparisons. Military spending is estimated to be more than $12.3 billion for 2002-2003, making Canada the sixth highest military spender within NATO, and the sixteenth highest in the world.

- The defence and foreign policies need to be reviewed publicly. Canada's defence policy as articulated in the 1994 White Paper on Defence Policy is woefully outdated and mired in Cold War thinking, while U.N. peacekeeping has been nearly abandoned by the Canadian Forces.

- Current defence dollars are being wasted and mismanaged. Billions of dollars have been spent on unnecessary military equipment and capabilities such as the faulty British submarines, unused pilot training and communications equipment, the unnecessary Joint Strike Fighter, and other programs.

- Defence policy and spending are being driven by special interests. A small, well-organized and well-funded defence lobby in Canada and the United States is driving the public debate on defence spending, despite Canadian public opinion dramatically desiring the federal government to focus on social programs – not military spending.

The pressure to increase Canada's military spending is an ever-present factor in Canadian politics, a position championed by a defence lobby comprising retired generals, security think tanks, academics, and corporations that benefit from military contracts.

But in the wake of the terrorist attacks on the United States on September 11th, the Bush Administration has joined Canada's defence lobby in calling for increases of billions of dollars to Canada's military spending. Emboldened by the heightened public concern about security and the ongoing War on Terrorism, the defence lobby is pressing its case on the federal government to redirect revenues to the military, even at the expense of Canada's social programs such as health care.

To date, the debate has been largely between the government and the defence lobby. The views of citizens are generally overlooked, despite the fact that polling shows that Canadians overwhelmingly want scarce tax dollars to go to social programs like health care and education (72 per cent) - not defence (only 7 per cent).

A review of Canada's Department of National Defence reveals that the department's problems do not stem from insufficient funding, but from a flawed and outdated defence policy forged nearly a decade ago, and a long history of poor planning, waste and mismanagement of Canadians' defence dollars.

The outdated defence policy and pressure from the United States and NATO have resulted in Canadian Forces trying to play an increasingly combat-oriented role internationally. These missions under NATO and U.S. command have come at the expense of traditional U.N. peacekeeping, so much so that at the end of 2001 only 219 soldiers - fewer than six per cent of deployed Canadian personnel - were participating in U.N. peacekeeping missions.

Increases in military spending now would reward the waste and mismanagement of defence dollars. The last decade has witnessed billions of dollars misspent on big-ticket military programs with no clear purpose or benefit to Canada's defence - for example, $750 million wasted on used British submarines with a well-known history of design flaws, $174 million on a satellite communication system that was never used, $65 million for pilot training that was never taken, and generous raises for generals and admirals while privates suffered a wage freeze for eight years.

Other factors unrelated to defence policy have also driven up military spending. Military spending and participation in the U.S.-led War on Terrorism are being used to curry favour with the United States, Canada's largest trading partner. A growing number of Canadian corporations receiving multi-million dollar contracts from DND are lobbying for more contracts. And free trade agreements that limit government powers are driving defence dollars toward corporate subsidies and other non-defence economic purposes.

Economic globalization is creating conditions for conflict and generating the demand for the military protection of economic interests. It is deepening the root causes of wars, such as environmental degradation and inequality. As Western economic interests become dependent upon far-flung investments, Western militaries will be called upon to defend those economic interests.

Canadians are resisting Canada's participation in the War on Terrorism and more military spending, which will come at the expense of social programs. Polls are telling the government that Canadians desire Canada to take an independent role from the United States, to seek non-military means to effect positive change in the world, and to protect Canadian sovereignty and social programs.

Introduction

The issue of defence spending has once again returned to the front pages of the newspapers as Canada prepares a new federal budget. In the wake of September 11th and the ensuing War on Terrorism, many commentators and research organizations are calling on Defence Minister John McCallum to dramatically increase defence spending.

> **"Breaking Rank: A citizens' review of Canada's defence** *spending has been prepared to provide the government with an alternate view: that there should not be any increase in Canada's military spending..."*

One of the most influential voices is Parliament's own Standing Committee on National Defence and Veterans Affairs (SCONDVA), which released a report entitled *Facing our Responsibilities: The State of Readiness of the Canadian Forces* in May 2002.[1] The report included twenty-five recommendations to the government, with the most prominent recommendation calling for increasing defence spending by nearly 50 per cent, raising the defence budget by $6 billion within three years.

The all-party committee's report was supported by committee members from all four national political parties: the Liberal Party, the Progressive Conservative Party, the Canadian Alliance, and the New Democratic Party, with a dissenting report submitted by the Bloc Québecois.

However, the debate on whether Canada should increase military spending has been very one-sided. The federal government has not been presented with the view of the majority of Canadians that defence spending, while necessary in principle, must be weighed against more important priorities such as health care and education.

Even more, the United States' massive restructuring of its security and military forces into a Department of Homeland Security along with the creation of Northern

---

1   Facing our Responsibilities: The State of Readiness of the Canadian Forces, Standing Committee on National Defence and Veterans Affairs, May 2002, http://www.parl.gc.ca/InfoComDoc/37/1/NDVA/Studies/Reports/ndvarp04-e.htm.

Command is pressuring Canada to adopt higher levels of military spending, harmonized laws on border controls and immigration, and increased police powers that limit civil liberties.

In response to the SCONDVA report and media attention to the issue, Minister of Defence McCallum initiated a low-level, internal update of Canada's defence program.[2] The result of this review will form the basis of input into the federal budget, expected in February 2003. But like the flawed SCONDVA report, the minister is only hearing from the defence lobby.

Breaking Rank: A citizens' review of Canada's defence spending has been prepared to provide the government with an alternate view: that there should not be any increase in Canada's military spending and the government should return to reducing the budget through an improved, less expensive defence policy. The resulting savings should be used to rebuild and expand social programs that have been seriously eroded since the federal spending cuts of the mid-1990s.

---

2   To visit the Defence Update Consultation Site, go to http://www.forces.gc.ca/menu/consult/ index_e.asp.

September 11th and the War on Terrorism

The immeasurable effect of the terrorist attacks on September 11th gave tremendous momentum to several domestic political trends that were already in motion before the attacks. For example, military spending in industrialized countries, including the United States and Canada, was already on the rise; the proposed National Missile Defence system was an international controversy; and border issues and Canadian access to U.S. markets were daily news items in Canadian newspapers. Moreover, the global economy was already faltering and showing signs of a slow-down.

Photo by Cpl Lou Penney.

The 3rd Battalion of Princess Patricia's Canadian Light Infantry Battle Group marches past the Canadian and American flags in Afghanistan at Kandahar Airport. The troops were a part of Canada's contribution to the War on Terrorism.

Advocates for action on all of these issues suddenly found that the terrorist attacks had cleared away political obstacles to their defence, foreign policy, and economic agendas. The Bush Administration in particular grasped its new moral authority to pursue its proposed military build-up – even taking the United States into a budget deficit to pay for new military spending and tax cuts.

Today, the momentum continues as the U.S. has reversed decades of military doctrine and adopted a national security policy that includes the use of preemptive attacks against foes – real or perceived. This reversal allows the United States to attack with little or no direct provocation, and its first employment of this policy is being directed at Iraq.

In Canada too, the September 11th attacks are being used to justify many initiatives – especially those that harmonize Canadian policies with those of the United States in areas such as immigration and border controls and defence policy. Many

Canadians – and even Liberal Members of Parliament – are becoming increasingly concerned that the federal government is surrendering too much sovereignty in order to assuage U.S. security fears.

However, other elements of the federal government are using the attacks as justification for a pro-defence spending agenda. The Standing Committee on National Defence and Veterans Affairs (SCONDVA) released a report in May 2002 that specifically cited the U.S.-led War on Terrorism as justifying a dramatic increase in defence spending.

The military response to the September 11th attacks begs the question: Will additional military spending increase Canadians' security?

There is little evidence to suggest that a larger military with more modern weaponry will improve Canadians' security, given that Canada faces little threat of terrorist attack and conventional forces are generally accepted as being ineffective against terrorism. In fact, boosting military spending to prevent terrorism is like building more prisons to fight crime - the response only deals with the problem after the worst effects are felt, rather than addressing the root causes.

The impotence of the traditional military view of security underscores the need for security planners to reassess Canadian security needs. Security should include Canadians' access to effective health care, safe food, and a clean environment. For example, the federal government's retreat from food testing and the heavy reliance on corporate adherence to voluntary standards leave Canadians vulnerable. As the world-renowned aquatic ecologist Dr. David Schindler has remarked, "What poses a greater risk to Canadians' health: terrorist attacks, or e-coli in their drinking water?"

But the defence lobby is now putting its demands before the government in the starkest of terms. A news report on a meeting with Defence Minister John McCallum in *The Ottawa Citizen* ran with the headline, "Focus on social programs will slow defence spending, lobbyists fear."[3] The defence lobby is working against broader

---

Table 1.

Poll: Canadians on Taxes and Spending

Spending Priorities:	Agree with most:
Priority should go to health because sick people have great needs.	41%
Priority should go to education because it's key to our future.	31%
In the violent world after September 11th, 2001, priority should go to defence and security against terrorism.	**7%**

Source: Compas Inc. April 2002

---

3   Naumetz, Tim; "PM's agenda ignores Forces, critics charge: Retirement delay, focus on social programs will slow defence spending, lobbyists fear," *The Ottawa Citizen* 28 August 2002, A5.

public opinion, given that Canadians consistently emphasize a focus on the economy, health care and education as top priorities for their political leaders, placing defence far down the list when asked to rank the issues.

In April, Canadians told pollsters that they expected the federal government to not divert its attention from social priorities such as health care and education. A Compas Inc. poll for Can-West Southam newspapers, Global TV and *The National Post* asked Canadians what principles should guide government program spending. Seventy-two per cent said health care or education should be a top priority. But only seven per cent agreed that "In the violent world after September 11th, 2001, priority should go to defence and security against terrorism."[4]

---

4   "Canadians on Taxes and Spending", *Compas Inc.* 29 April 2002, http://www.compas.ca/html/arhcives/taxesandspending_surv.html.

Canada's High Level of Military Spending

In the current political climate, it may seem heretical to suggest that Canada is already a high military spender. Nevertheless, that is the case when one looks at the actual dollar amounts Canada spends each year on operating and arming its military.

In fact, Canada is one of the largest military spenders in the world and ranks very highly within NATO's 19-member alliance. While budget figures and actual spending estimate figures will vary, in the current fiscal year of 2002-03, the Department of National Defence will spend $12.318 billion.[5] Using the Department of National Defence's own figures, this places Canada as the sixth highest within NATO's nineteen members, and the sixteenth highest military spender in the world.[6]

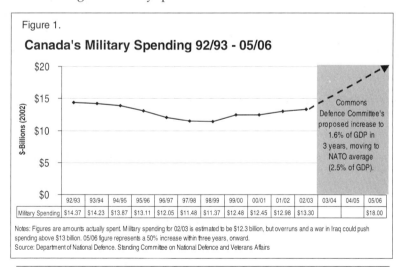

Figure 1.

Canada's Military Spending 92/93 - 05/06

Military Spending	92/93	93/94	94/95	95/96	96/97	97/98	98/99	99/00	00/01	01/02	02/03	03/04	04/05	05/06
	$14.37	$14.23	$13.87	$13.11	$12.05	$11.48	$11.37	$12.48	$12.45	$12.98	$13.30			$18.00

Commons Defence Committee's proposed increase to 1.6% of GDP in 3 years, moving to NATO average (2.5% of GDP).

Notes: Figures are amounts actually spent. Military spending for 02/03 is estimated to be $12.3 billion, but overruns and a war in Iraq could push spending above $13 billion. 05/06 figure represents a 50% increase within three years, onward.
Source: Department of National Defence. Standing Committee on National Defence and Veterans Affairs

5   Reports on Plans and Priorities 2002-2003, Department of National Defence, Table 3: Gross Planned Spending. p. 39. This figure includes all spending by the Department of National Defence, which includes money derived from sources other than the federal government. Military spending figures are used throughout the report, except where it is noted that budget figures are being used.
6   Defence Update Consultation Site: Defence Portfolio. Department of National Defence, http://www.forces.gc.ca/menu/consult/current_policy/defence_portfolio/section_10_e.asp.

Dissatisfied with Canada's military spending, the Standing Committee on National Defence and Veterans Affairs (SCONDVA) issued its report "Facing our Responsibilities" in May, with the recommendation that "the government increase the annual base budget for the Department of National Defence to between 1.5% to 1.6% of GDP (Gross Domestic Product), with the increase to be phased in over the next three years, and continue to move towards the NATO average."[7]

Given that Canada's military spending of more than $12 billion is 1.1 per cent of its GDP, this recommendation is actually calling for an increase in annual military spending of nearly 50 per cent, or $6 billion within three years (an additional $2 billion every year for three years). With the NATO average of military budgets at 2.5 per cent of GDP, the committee's recommendation would more than double Canada's military spending before the end of the decade, putting it at nearly $28 billion – higher than it has ever been in history.

> Box 1.
> ## Measurements of military spending
> ### *The Budget or Total Spending*
> "Total spending" is the figure most commonly cited for the Department of National Defence's (DND) budget. The figure is always lower than the overall amount DND spends because it includes only the amount directly budgeted for the department by the federal government. DND has other revenue sources, such as the rental of bases and facilities, pilot training for foreign militaries, etc., that supplement this budget.
>
> ### *Estimates of Gross Spending*
> "Gross spending" is a more accurate measurement of the overall amount DND will spend in a given budget year because it includes all of DND's sources of revenue. Estimates of both "total" and "gross" spending are published for each budget year by the Treasury Board in the annual departmental Report on Plans and Priorities document.
>
> ### *Actual Spending*
> "Actual spending" is the final figure spent by DND at the end of each budget year. Most of the spending calculations in this report are based on actual gross spending figures. This is always the highest figure, because it includes all revenues and any mid-year increases, such as extra funds to pay for unexpected military operations. In recent years, the actual amount spent has often been more than $500 million higher than originally estimated (see Table 2).

The Defence Lobby's Luxembourg Deception

It has been so often repeated by the defence lobby – and increasingly by the news media – it is becoming a truism that "Canada's military spending is as low as Luxembourg's as a percentage of GDP."[8] But this statistic is intentionally misleading, and doesn't tell the truth about Canada's or global military spending.

Table 2.
Canada's Military Spending (2002 $billions)

Year	Planned	Actual	Difference
98-99	$10.58	$11.37	+ $0.79
99-00	$11.68	$12.48	+ $0.81
00-01	$11.84	$12.45	+ $0.60
01-02	$12.32	$12.98	+ $0.66

---

7   Facing our Responsibilities: The State of Readiness of the Canadian Forces, Standing Committee on National Defence and Veterans Affairs, May 2002. http://www.parl.gc.ca/InfoComDoc/37/1/NDVA/Studies/Reports/ndvarp04-e.htm.

8   "MPs challenge McCallum to raise defence spending," *The Globe and Mail*, 28 May 02, A1.

When calculated using actual dollars, Canada's $12.3 billion in military spending is more than that of most of the other NATO members, including Spain, the Netherlands and Turkey – and three times as much as that of Denmark and Belgium.

Describing Canada's military spending as a percentage of GDP is used by members of the defence lobby to make Canada's military spending seem very low in order to build an argument for more military spending.

Using the 2001 figures below, at 1.1 per cent of its GDP, Canada does in fact appear to spend as little as Luxembourg, which spends 0.8 per cent of its GDP.

Table 3.

NATO Defence Budgets as per cent (%) of GDP versus Actual Budget (2001)*

NATO Defence Budgets as per cent (%) of GDP (2001)			NATO Defence Budgets as Actual Dollars (2001)		
Rank	NATO Country	% GDP	Rank	NATO Country	$billions (U.S.)
1	Turkey	5.0	1	United States	310.5
2	Greece	4.8	2	United Kingdom	34.0
3	United States	2.9	3	France	25.3
4	France	2.6	4	Germany	21.0
5	United Kingdom	2.4	5	Italy	15.5
6	Czech Republic	2.2	6	Canada	7.3
7	Portugal	2.1	7	Spain	6.9
8	Italy	1.9	8	Netherlands	5.6
9	Poland	1.8	9	Turkey	5.1
10	Norway	1.8	10	Poland	3.7
11	Hungary	1.8	11	Greece	3.3
12	Netherlands	1.6	12	Norway	2.8
13	Denmark	1.5	13	Denmark	2.4
14	Germany	1.5	14	Belgium	2.2
15	Belgium	1.3	15	Portugal	1.3
16	Spain	1.2	16	Czech Republic	1.1
17	Canada	1.1	17	Hungary	0.8
18	Luxembourg	0.8	18	Luxembourg	0.1
19	Iceland	0.0	19	Iceland	0.0

Source: Department of National Defence[9]
*Note that these figures are best used for comparison purposes only. Figures used elsewhere in this report provide more accurate military spending figures in 2002 Canadian dollars.

9   Defence Update Consultation Site: Defence Portfolio. Department of National Defence, http://www.forces.gc.ca/menu/consult/current_policy/defence_portfolio/section_10_e.asp.

But incredibly, the same figures also indicate that Turkey and Greece spend more than the United States. The shortcomings of this method become immediately apparent when by comparison, we see that in actual dollars the United States spent a whopping $310.2 billion (U.S.), and Turkey only $5.1 billion (U.S.). Obviously, therefore, this method does not give an accurate picture of which countries spend the most or least on their militaries, and anyone who uses this method is open to challenge.

The "peace dividend" is being clawed back.

The Progressive Conservative Member of Parliament for Saint John, Elsie Wayne, complained in *The Ottawa Citizen* that since the Conservatives lost the 1993 election to the Liberals, the latter have made unwarranted cuts to defence. She said, "Since the Liberals took power in late 1993, it is very clear they consider defence spending to be a disposable luxury, not a priority."[10]

However, Wayne's championing of Cold War-level military spending may be heavily influenced by the presence of defence industries in her riding. Saint John includes the Irving-owned Saint John Ship Building, the corporation that received the lion's share of billions of dollars in defence contracts to build the Navy's patrol frigates and maritime coastal defence vessels in the 1980s and 1990s.

Canada's defence spending was quite properly reduced with the end of the Cold War. The 20 per cent reduction in spending, the closing of bases, and the reduction of uniformed personnel was an entirely reasonable response to the end of the East-West standoff.[11]

It is noteworthy that even with these reductions, Canada's military spending has still not dropped below the spending levels prior to the early 1980s. Canada's military spending in 1980-81 was $10.3 billion (in 2002 dollars), making planned 2002-03 spending 19 per cent higher than it was before the Mulroney and Reagan-era military build-ups.

As in Canada, military spending is marching upwards throughout the world. This regrettable rise in global military spending is documented in the 2001 United Nations Disarmament Yearbook, which noted spending increased both globally and in most regions, reaching nearly $840 billion in 2001.[12] In the aftermath of September 11th this trend will certainly continue.

---

10 Wayne, Elsie; "Martin must reveal Armed Forces Policy," *The Ottawa Citizen*, 23 July 2002, A13.
11 The Department of National Defence states that its budget was reduced by 23 per cent between 1993-94 and 1998-99. However, actual 1998-99 military spending was approximately $700 million higher than the 1998-99 budgeted amount. Using actual spending and calculating inflation on the basis of the GDP deflator, the real reduction in spending was about 20 per cent.
12 "Countries spent nearly $840 billion in 2001 on military, U.N. reports," *U.N. News Service*, 1 August 2002.

Canada's Expensive War-making Defence Policy

Defence Minister John McCallum has placed the issue of defence spending within a debate on Canada's defence policy. In a July 2002 CBC Radio interview, McCallum was asked what arguments he will make to Cabinet to increase Canada's $12.3-billion military spending. McCallum replied:

> "I think there's two real options. One, we provide some additional resources so that we can do what we are currently doing on a sustainable [basis]. Or, if the government doesn't...isn't willing to put in those additional resources, we have to figure out ways to do less."[13]

Defence Minister McCallum's comments illustrate the relationship between defence policy and spending: the defence policy lays out expected defence capabilities, and the defence budget should provide sufficient resources to satisfy the policy. The solution, as McCallum points out, is to provide more money or change the policy.

Photo by Sgt Dennis Mah

The CH-149 Cormorant search-and-rescue helicopter can lift a payload of 5,000 kilograms, and has room for 40 passengers or 12 stretchers. These helicopters are estimated to cost about half as much as the naval warfare helicopters for the patrol frigates.

Canada's current defence policy is outdated and mired in Cold War thinking. The current policy was laid out in the 1994 White Paper on Defence Policy, which set out the government's vision for the Canadian Forces: its mission, priorities, and capabilities. The 1994 White Paper was controversial at the time because it was the first defence policy since the end of the Cold War, so it was mired in an internal conflict between the three branches of the armed forces which were all positioning themselves to avoid cuts to defence spending. The result was a policy that took

---

13   "John McCallum comments on Canadian troops," *CBC Radio Transcripts*, 23 July 2002.

> **"This policy of maintaining and equipping 'multi-purpose, combat-capable forces' is very expensive and unrealistic."**

few initiatives and departed little from previous policies.

Significantly, however, the 1994 White Paper reaffirmed that Canada would maintain armed forces capable of waging wars beyond Canada's own immediate defence needs – and far beyond peacekeeping. In the debate on whether or not the Canadian Forces should adjust to the end of the Cold War and focus on sovereignty patrols and lightly armed peacekeeping, the 1994 White Paper on Defence Policy concluded: "The retention of multi-purpose, combat-capable forces represents the only prudent choice for Canada."[14]

This policy of maintaining and equipping "multi-purpose, combat-capable forces" is very expensive and unrealistic. During public hearings held on defence and foreign policy in 1993, a blue ribbon panel of security experts calling themselves the Canada 21 Council issued a report advocating a peacekeeping-oriented policy that was less entrenched in Cold War thinking.

The Canada 21 report stated:

> "The Council does not believe that there is any likely threat to Canada from the submarines or bombers of any foreign state, and proposes that Canada choose to abstain from any international operations that include the possibility of attacks by heavy armoured formations, heavy artillery, or modern airpower."[15]

The report went on to sensibly recommend that the Canadian Forces cease buying equipment and phase out existing equipment to counter these threats. This included dropping Canada's anti-submarine warfare role, not purchasing new submarines, and reducing Canada's fighter aircraft fleet by two-thirds.

Today – eight years after the debate over the 1994 White Paper – some military planners are coming to agree with the Canada 21 Council's view that the "multi-purpose, combat-capable" forces are a waste of money, given Canada's defence needs.

David King, a former Colonel in the Canadian Forces who is currently a faculty member at the U.S. Defense University in Washington, D.C., wrote in the April 2002 issue of *Policy Options* magazine:

> "The 'general purpose fully combat-capable forces' cliché that currently informs [Canada's] defence organization is in fact not very well related to the nation's needs. In the current policy environment a funding increase would be a further waste."[16]

---

14 1994 White Paper on Defence Policy, http://www.forces.gc.ca/admpol/pol_docs/94wp/white_paper_94.html.

15 Canada 21: Canada and Common Security in the Twenty-First Century. Centre for International Studies, University of Toronto, 1994, p. 64.

16 King, David L.; "We need a Romanow Commission for Defence and Foreign Policy," *Policy Options*, April 2002, Vol. 23 No 03.

The Military's Abandonment of U.N. Peacekeeping

Many Canadians support the traditional peacekeeping role of the Canadian Forces. Since the Pearson era, our military has delivered Canada's "middle-power" foreign policy and commitment to the United Nations through non-combat peacekeeping. These operations around the world have seen the trademark Canadian peacekeepers: lightly armed and wearing the U.N.'s blue berets. These neutral peacekeepers worked with both groups of previously warring parties to bring a lasting end to the conflict.

Canadian soldiers distributing toys in Bosnia. Photos like this have been used to promote the Canadian Forces to the public, but undermine support for the military's involvement in war, say analysts.

Sadly, the image of the Canadian military acting in U.N.-sponsored peacekeeping missions is all but a myth today. In this regard, Canada is hardly participating in U.N. peacekeeping missions at all. According to the Department of National Defence, at the end of 2001 Canada had a mere 219 personnel participating in U.N. missions out of 3,775 personnel deployed around the world. This means that nearly 95 per cent of military personnel were either deployed as part of the war against Afghanistan or with NATO missions in Bosnia, while only 5.8 per cent supported U.N. missions.[17]

The military's financial commitment to U.N. peacekeeping is even smaller than its personnel commitment. The estimated incremental costs to Canada of U.N. peacekeeping missions in 2002-2003 will be $10.2 million (i.e. costs incurred because of the U.N. mission, and not including the ongoing costs of training and equipping soldiers,

---

17 Report on Plans and Priorities 2002, Department of National Defence, pages 55-57, http://
www.vcds.forces.gc.ca/dgsp/dfppc/pubs/rpp01/00native/rpp-2002-2003_e.pdf.

> "...the peacekeeping image has been so successful that the Canadian public largely doesn't recognize the fact that the military is primarily a war-fighting organization"

etc.). But even that is not the total cost, since the U.N. reimburses Canada for its peacekeeping missions. This refund will further reduce the total cost to DND for peacekeeping missions to $2.3 million – or only .02 of one per cent of total Canadian military spending in 2002-2003.

Canada's role in U.N. peacekeeping missions is an issue of great debate inside the defence establishment. On the one hand, some view peacekeeping as undermining the military's war-fighting capability by risking further spending cuts to support a mere "constabulary" force. On the other hand, some view peacekeeping as generating a positive image that can build public support for the Canadian Forces and its large budget, which as shown above is really used to pay for non-U.N. combat missions.

A March 2001 report from a meeting convened by DND to bring together sixty-five defence experts to discuss Canadian defence policy illustrated this debate:

> "One participant raised the concern that the Canadian military is losing its character and war-fighting capability by becoming too involved in PSO [Peace Support Operations], and cautioned that the Canadian myth of the CF [Canadian Forces] as peacekeepers and not war-fighters has to be broken in order to salvage the primary purpose of the CF...Yet another participant remarked that including phrases such as 'war-fighting' in public communications results in reduced support from the public for such operations, even if the label is more accurate."[18]

Mercedes Stephenson, President of the Society for Military and Strategic Studies at the University of Calgary, points out that the Department of National Defence and the government have used the peacekeeping image to build public support for defence spending and the military in general.

Stephenson wrote in June 2002 in *Defence Policy Review* that the peacekeeping image has been so successful that the Canadian public largely doesn't recognize the fact that the military is primarily a war-fighting organization:

> "The image of the good boy scout Canadian Forces soldier confused the public about what the role of the Canadian Forces actually is. Peacekeeping is an honourable cause, but it is not the primary mission of the military."[19]

---

18 Department of National Defence Consultation Report: Future Canadian Defence Policy, DND Directorate of Public Policy, 23 March 2001, p.4, http://www.forces.gc.ca/admpol/org/dg_coord/d_pub/sdf/reports/cu01_forum_e.htm.

19 Stephenson, Mercedes; "A fresh look at military-media relationships," Defence Policy Review, 17 June, 2002. p. 3.

In other words, without the reassuring peacekeeping image the Canadian public may not be inclined to support the high levels of defence spending demanded by a defence policy that goes beyond peacekeeping to field aggressive, "multi-purpose, combat-capable" armed forces.

This "disconnect" between image and reality is becoming more apparent to the Canadian public as traditional peacekeeping disappears. The military's "boy scout" image crumbled when Canadian soldiers tortured and killed a 16-year-old boy during a peacekeeping mission in Somalia. As Stephenson described it, "The Canadian government left the public to scratch its head over how *Leave it to Beaver* had turned into *Apocalypse Now*."[20]

The departure from the traditional peacekeeping role began in 1991 when Canadian CF-18s escorted coalition bombers over Iraq during the Gulf War. This escalated when Canada contributed eighteen CF-18s to bombing operations against the former Yugoslavia under NATO – not U.N. – command in 1999. Canadian planes flew 682 sorties and dropped 530 bombs, of which 361 were laser-guided bombs.

The Canadian Forces were also deployed in Afghanistan to fight a ground war under U.S. command. This is a stark departure from the lightly armed peacekeeping role Canada proudly played in trouble spots like Cyprus for many years.

---

20 Ibid.

Globalization and Terrorism

Globalization, free trade agreements, and international financial institutions such as the World Trade Organization (WTO), the World Bank and the International Monetary Fund are contributing to the root causes of terrorism and insecurity around the world. Canada, as an important and influential member of these organizations, is by extension more part of the problem than part of the solution.

Globalization creates a breeding ground for terrorism.

A young girl in the village of Molla Abdulla Kariz, Afghanistan, peaks around the corner to watch as a Canadian and American patrol moves through her town for the first time.

Canada's foreign and trade policies are supporting a global economy that limits the power of governments to intervene in their own domestic economies. Free trade agreements, such as those negotiated and enforced by the World Trade Organization, are undermining the ability of the governments in the developing world to enact policies that avert conflict and environmental degradation. These countries are in the very same regions that may spawn terrorism and collapse into civil wars where Canadian Forces may be later called to participate in war or peacekeeping operations.

Canada's international trade policy supports the expansion of trade liberalization and deregulation through these free trade agreements. Canada plays a leading role in the World Trade Organization and Canada's foreign policy is increasingly dominated by the trade agenda.

Columnist Murray Dobbin has described the changing view of Canada by people in the developing world: "When Canadian non-governmental organizations meet with their counterparts in international forums, they brace themselves for the

19

inevitable question: How can Canada have abandoned its historic, positive role to become one of the world's most aggressive pushers of free market policies?"[21]

The United Nations has been critical of these free trade agreements because they reduce each government's ability to provide the essential social programs that alleviate the conditions conducive to war and armed conflict. The 1999 U.N. Human Development Report stated that "globalization is creating new threats to human security – in rich countries and poor" by creating insecurity in areas of finance, jobs and income, health, culture, the environment, and even personal, political and community security.[22]

> *"...globalization is creating new threats to human security – in rich countries and poor"*

Moreover, globalization's toll on the environment and the demand for limited resources is a new cause of conflict. In 1995, World Bank Vice-President Ismail Serageldin told *Newsweek* that "Many of the wars this century were about oil, but those of the next century will be over water."

More recently Michael Klare, an expert on armed conflict at Hampshire College in Amherst, Massachusetts, wrote that this century will see the rise of "resource wars." In his book of the same title, Klare clearly draws the link between globalization's most damaging effects in the Third World and its incitement of impoverished people to accept fundamentalism and extremism – the root causes of terrorism.

Klare writes:

> "The risk of internal conflict is further heightened by the growing divide between the rich and the poor in many developing countries – a phenomenon widely ascribed to globalization. As supplies contract and the price of many materials rises, the poor will find themselves in an increasingly desperate situation – and thus more inclined to heed the exhortations of demagogues, fundamentalists, and extremists who promise to relieve their suffering through revolt or ethnic partition."[23]

Or by flying planes into office towers.

The military is being used to defend globalization.

Do Canada's national security interests include economic interests as well?

According to the federal government, Canada's economic security depends upon the continued expansion of trade liberalization through instruments such as the World Trade Organization, the Free Trade Area of the Americas, and bilateral free

---

21 Dobbin, Murray; "Canada is a World Class Trade Bully," *Financial Post,* 12 November 2002.

22 Human Development Report 1999, United Nations Development Programme, Oxford University Press, New York, 1999, p. 3-5.

23 Klare, Michael; *Resource Wars: The New Landscape of Global Conflict,* New York: Metropolitan/Owl, 2001. p. 24.

trade agreements. It would therefore follow that free trade and globalization are essential components of national security.

This means that the government could easily define the defence of Canada's national economic security as the defence of globalization itself. Likewise, nations, organizations, and even individuals who challenge the unimpeded expansion of economic globalization could thus be seen as national security threats.

Canadian CF-18s deployed in Italy under Operation Echo participated in the NATO bombing campaign over the former Republic of Yugoslavia.

This is certainly the view of the U.S. administration. U.S. President Bush's National Security Strategy of the United States of America released in September 2002 very clearly draws the connecting lines between the free use of military power and free trade – declaring them both essential to national interests.[24] To many observers, this strategy has been elevated to the level of a doctrine that will define U.S. military and economic power well into the century.

Canada's 1994 White Paper on Defence Policy similarly identified links between the economic system and the use of military power. The Canadian Forces are responsible for defending Canadian interests in light of the spreading of these economic interests around the world. The 1994 White Paper states:

> "As a nation that throughout its history has done much within the context of international alliances to defend freedom and democracy, Canada continues to have a vital interest in doing its part to ensure global security, especially since Canada's economic future depends on its ability to trade freely with other nations."[25]

But with globalization spreading Canada's economic interests around the world and our economy becoming integrated into the global economy, which is led by the Western industrialized countries, the defence of Canada's interests may require Canadian Forces fighting wars to defend corporate investment and interests. Could the War on Terrorism be used to wage wars to gain or maintain access to oil or other resources in regions like the Middle East, or to defend corporate investments in Latin American countries such as Colombia?

---

24 "The National Security Strategy of the United States of America," The White House, Washington, D.C., September 2002.

25 1994 White Paper on Defence Policy Highlights, http://www.forces.gc.ca/admpol/pol_docs/94wp/highlights.html.

In a word, yes – according to the defence lobby and corporations. Corporations and economic elites are depending on the military to defend their corporate interests around the world, and even here at home. The Conference of Defence Associations, a front group for the defence lobby, articulated this view in a report released in 2000. The report, which was funded by the Business Council on National Issues, the Molson Foundation, and even the Department of National Defence itself, called for more military spending to defend free trade. It argued:

> "The defence establishment, including the Canadian Forces, plays a key role in an international policy which provides the insurance and the means which allow the national interest to flourish. It contributes to stability at home and abroad, thus supporting the development of an environment congenial to trade."[26]

While defending corporate interests abroad, even more sinister may be the role the military will play at home. The Department of National Defence has been given additional powers through Canada's new anti-terrorism laws to provide security forces around international meetings in Canada. Civil liberties organizations have pointed to these powers as being directed at legitimate critics of globalization and the policies of the Canadian government, thereby undermining Canadians' inherent right to freedom of expression.

International trade meetings provide opportunities for governments and corporations to come together to further globalization, such as the recent Summit of the Americas in Quebec City and the G-8 meeting in Kananaskis. Since the public outcry at the WTO meeting in Seattle in 1999, these international meetings have become a focal point for the growing anti-globalization movement where tens of thousands of citizens gather to demonstrate their opposition to the global economy.

Fuelled with the millions of additional dollars given to spy agencies such as the Canadian Security Intelligence Service (CSIS), the Communication Security Establishment, and the RCMP, all of Canada's security forces will be using additional legislative powers to limit democratic dissent. If the pre-emptive arrests, entrapment operations, and surveillance by security forces of activists and journalists during the Summit of the Americas meeting in Quebec City in April of 2001 are any indication, Canadians should be very concerned.

---

26 Stability and Prosperity: The Benefits of Investment in Defence, The Conference of Defence Associations Institute, Ottawa, 2000.

Mismanagement and Waste of Defence Dollars

Canada's defence policy is unsound because it has failed to adjust to the post-Cold War world. As a result, the military is wasting money on ill-conceived arms programs and unnecessary capabilities designed to fight improbable conflicts and fulfill the adventurous "multi-purpose, combat-capable forces" mission from the 1994 White Paper on Defence Policy. Other

> *"Canada's defence policy is unsound because it has failed to adjust to the post-Cold War world. "*

programs have little to do with defence policy at all, and were funded to provide contracts to politically or economically important corporations.

Despite the end of the Cold War, which eliminated the purpose of many of DND's projects, billions of dollars are being spent with no clear benefit to the military. Even more, jobs vanish after the projects end and waste the potential for investment and job creation in programs that could make a long-term contribution to the economy or public service. For example, public transportation systems and environmental technologies have longer-term benefits to the economy than the production of warships, missiles, and military helicopters.

NATO Flight Training in Canada

The Department of National Defence has undertaken a widespread program of privatization of non-combat services. DND's showcase privatized program is the NATO Flight Training in Canada, which provides fighter pilot training to Canadians and pilots from several European and Asian militaries in Moose Jaw, Saskatchewan.

Canada's Auditor General has criticized NATO Flight Training in Canada since the program was established in 1998. The NATO Flight Training Centre was created through a 20-year, $2.8-billion non-competitive contract awarded to a consortium of aerospace and defence corporations led by Montreal-based Bombardier.

The then-Auditor General, Denis Desautels, criticized the project in 1999 because the contract with Bombardier was non-competitive, it guaranteed $200 million in profits to Bombardier, which is excessive for this kind of contract, and the complicated nature of the contract unnecessarily increased the risk to the Canadian government.[27]

Four years into the project, the Auditor General once again documented a waste of military spending in the program. Sheila Fraser's October 2002 report to Parliament revealed that DND had paid Bombardier $65 million for pilot training never used. In fact, the contract signed by DND provides Bombardier with regular payments without adequate evaluation of the corporation's performance.

The Patrol Frigate Program

Photo by MCpl Pierre Vaudry.

The HMCS Ottawa is one of 12 frigates built for the Canadian Navy at a cost of $9 billion. These ships often visit Third World countries to promote Canadian arms sales. Some defence experts believe Canada has too many frigates and want some mothballed.

In 1977, twelve patrol frigates were ordered from shipyards in New Brunswick and Quebec for the Canadian Navy at an estimated cost of $1.5 billion. In defending the program, then-Finance Minister Jean Chrétien promised that jobs and exports would keep the shipyards busy for decades.

However, the cost of the ships and expensive repairs to correct design flaws pushed the final price tag of the program up to $9 billion. Furthermore, the high cost of the ships, poor performance, and the end of the Cold War ruined any hope of foreign sales after the original order was filled.[28]

Today, the thousands of jobs that were created are gone, and the ships are yet to be equipped with expensive helicopters and will soon require more expensive upgrades. Canada has too many frigates, which has prompted some defence officials to suggest mothballing a number of ships to redirect funds to other projects. Ironically, many defence experts have expressed concerns that Canada lacks sufficient numbers of ships to patrol the country's coastline, while the frigates are frequently sent to conduct port visits in Third World countries such as Indonesia to promote Canadian arms sales, or to enforce economic sanctions against Iraq in the Persian Gulf.

---

27 1999 Report of the Auditor General of Canada, http://www.oag-bvg.gc.ca/domino/reports.nsf/a1b15 d892a1f761a852565c40068a492/c1bdf2c11e7fb03a8525682e00622776?OpenDocument&Highlight =0,nato.

28 Trautman, Jim; "Military Surplus." *Report on Business* June 1999. p. 14.

The Maritime Helicopter Project

The $2.9-billion plan to buy twenty-eight ship-borne anti-submarine warfare helicopters to replace the Sea Kings on Canadian frigates has been the longest running equipment program in Canadian history, dating back to the 1980s. While much media attention has been paid to the need to replace the aging Sea Kings, there has been little public scrutiny of why the forces need helicopters with anti-submarine warfare capabilities designed to find Russian submarines, given that Russia is now an ally and cannot even afford to deploy submarines. Furthermore, if the patrol frigates themselves have no clear mission, then why should Canada spend so much on equipping all twelve ships with new helicopters?

The original helicopters ordered by the Mulroney Tories included a combination of search and rescue helicopters and ship-borne helicopters for the patrol frigates. The need for search and rescue helicopters was finally satisfied in the 1990s when Canada purchased fifteen land-based Cormorants for $790 million. These search and rescue helicopters are estimated to cost about half as much as the naval warfare helicopters for the patrol frigates.

Not only is the Maritime Helicopter Project expensive, it has become a contentious political issue between the Prime Minister's Office and the Department of National Defence. The Prime Minister's Office has accused the military of tilting the competition in favour of the controversial EH-101 helicopter, the same helicopter cancelled by the Liberals in 1993.

The Submarine Capability Life Extension (SCLE) Project

Photo by Alan Rowlands.

Canada's purchase of four decommissioned British submarines to replace the existing fleet of Oberon-class submarines has been plagued with mismanagement and waste. Canada agreed to purchase the four submarines for $750 million, ignoring a history of design problems including faulty torpedo doors, safety concerns with the power plant, and in one case, an obvious dent in the hull.[29]

The submarines now require expensive upgrades and repairs estimated to cost at least $1.4 million to repair the dent and

The HMCS Windsor, a used U.K. sub bought by Canada, leaves Britain for Halifax. The subs have flaws and require expensive repairs.

cracked valves. On top of that, the Navy wants to spend $250 million to install an air-independent propulsion system to give the submarines a "near nuclear" capability.

---

29 Pugliese, David; "Why Australia rejected Canada's 'new' submarines," *The Ottawa Citizen* 22 May 02, A1.

This means that they will be able to stay submerged for long periods of time, long enough to pass under the Polar Icecap. However, the projected cost of the refit is likely to be far too conservative a figure, as programs such as these often go wildly over-budget, as the Patrol Frigate Program has demonstrated.

These submarines have no clear purpose in Canadian defence needs that cannot be met by existing surface vessels – especially considering that the submarine threat has disappeared, thereby removing the need for an anti-submarine warfare capability. In fact, their most important function seems to be to allow the Canadian Navy to participate in war games with U.S. and British nuclear submarines, which are operated by crews that need to spar with quieter diesel-electric submarines like the Upholders.

The Very Long-Range Communication System (VLRCS)

In a further example of poor DND planning, the military spent $174 million to build a military satellite communication system that was never used. The system was completed in 1998, but has remained in storage since its delivery. This botched program was sharply criticized by the Auditor General of Canada, Sheila Fraser, in her April 2002 report to the House of Commons.[30]

The Joint Strike Fighter Program

Photo by Cpl Danielle Bernier.

A CF-18 armed with laser-guided bombs in Italy. DND is spending $1.2 billion to upgrade these fighters to use advanced and expensive U.S.-built weapons.

The defence lobby achieved a significant victory in 2002 when the Canadian government quietly announced that it would ante up $150 million (U.S.) to be part of the Pentagon's Joint Strike Fighter (JSF) program. Dubbed the "Jointly Spent Fortune" program by *The Economist* magazine, the multinational JSF program is the largest arms contract in history, worth an estimated $200 billion (U.S.) to develop and build 3000 planes.

The federal government's financial contribution will facilitate U.S. defence contracts being awarded to Canadian corporations since Canada is now an official participant in the JSF project. The government has established a high-powered committee of members from the Departments of Defence, Industry and Foreign Affairs to assist Canadian corporations in winning JSF contracts from the Pentagon.

However, the Canadian Forces has no plans to purchase this stealthy and offensive warplane, and is already spending nearly $1.2 billion to upgrade its existing fleet of CF-18s.

---

30 2002 Report of the Auditor General of Canada, April 2002, http://dsp-psd.communication.gc.ca/Collection/FA1-2002-1-0E.pdf.

The Canadian Cadet Program

The Canadian Cadet Program comprises some 56,000 Air Cadets, Army Cadets, and Sea Cadets in what DND promotes as the largest federally sponsored national youth training program for 12- to18-year-olds. However, while some of the leadership and other personal development skills taught to young people may be worthwhile, this program is also by far the most expensive national youth training program.

According to 2002-03 spending estimates, the Canadian Cadet Program will cost a substantial $155 million. By comparison, Scouts Canada and Girl Guides of Canada offer a similar program to 350,000 boys and girls at practically no cost at all to the federal government. In 1998, for example, Scouts Canada received no federal funding whatsoever, and Girl Guides receives about $25,000 in a typical year.

National Missile Defence

The next major defence program on the horizon is the Pentagon's ill-conceived National Missile Defense system – better known as Star Wars. The 2002 U.S. military budget includes $7.4 billion (U.S.) to continue developing the system for the next year. The system's ultimate cost defies estimates, but it is certainly in the tens if not hundreds of billions of dollars.

> **"While the federal government has not officially endorsed national missile defence, there is nothing preventing Canadian corporations from supplying U.S. defence contractors with components for the system."**

While the federal government has not officially endorsed national missile defence, there is nothing preventing Canadian corporations from supplying U.S. defence contractors with components for the system. In October 2002 the system's leading contactor, Boeing, announced a partnership with Toronto-based CAE Inc. in developing the missile defence system. The contract is part of a political strategy to undermine resistance to the program from allies. Similar agreements have been signed between Boeing and the U.K.'s BAE Systems, France and Germany's EADS, and Italy's Alenia Spazio.

The defence industry publication *Defense News* reported that "cooperation between the U.S. and British defense giants could be a blueprint for Washington's effort to secure support for missile defense: lure foreign firms with U.S. defense dollars and hope the contractors sway their governments to get on board."[31]

The Canadian government's political endorsement of the program, like the Joint Strike Fighter, will open the door to greater contracts for Canadian corporations as the Pentagon seeks to integrate Canada politically, militarily, and industrially into the program.

---

31 Chutter, Andrew, Gopal Rutnam and Jason Sherman; "Missile Defense: the new deal" *Defense News* 8 July 2002: p. 1.

Yet, any Canadian industry lobby for the government's endorsement of the missile defence system will fly in the face of widespread public opposition. In July 2001, a poll conducted by Ipsos-Reid found that a 58 per cent majority of Canadians said the government of Canada should oppose the U.S. building a missile defence system.[32]

Salaries and Working Conditions for Military Personnel

While billions of dollars were being spent on unneeded military equipment, stories of rank and file soldiers relying on foodbanks and part-time jobs to make ends meet made headlines across Canada in the late 1990s.

Adding even more insult to low-ranking personnel, whose salaries were frozen for eight years, high-ranking military brass enjoyed generous pay raises at the same time. According to documents obtained through the Access to Information Act by *The Ottawa Citizen*, between 1996 and 1998 salaries for the Canadian Forces' 35 brigadier-generals jumped 7.2 per cent to $90,989; the nearly 200 colonels got an average 4.6 per cent increase to $83,113; and the 22 major-generals and rear-admirals got raises of 5.8 per cent to $103,875.[33] Meanwhile, a private's salary ranged from $15,100 to $25,900 annually.

The low pay and poor living conditions for the average private serving in the Canadian Forces embarrassed the federal government into increasing military spending to provide salary increases and improvements to housing. In March 1999, then-Defence Minister Art Eggleton announced a series of pay raises for Canadian Forces personnel, including a 14.4 per cent increase to privates and a 7.28 per cent increase to non-commissioned officers, at a total cost of $1.9 billion over five years.[34]

For now, the issue of low salaries appears to have been addressed by the spending increases initiated in 1999. Advocates of increases in defence spending no longer cite low wages or living conditions to argue their case.

However, non-monetary issues such as poor personnel management by the military leadership continue to plague the Canadian Forces. According to a government survey released in the fall of 1999, 31 per cent of those surveyed said they had faced some form of harassment – sexual, racial or abuse of authority. This number is significantly higher than the overall public service average of 20 per cent. More than half of those surveyed would not recommend taking a job with the Canadian Forces.[35] With these kinds of problems within the military, it is little wonder that the Canadian Forces experience very low morale and continually fail to meet recruitment goals.

---

32 "Majority (58%) Oppose Missile Defence Shield," *Ipsos-Reid.* 23 July 2001, http://www.ipsos-reid.com/media/dsp_displaypr_cdn.cfm?id_to_view=1265.

33 Blanchfield, Mike; "Troops struggled to make ends meet, while brass enjoyed raises," The *Globe and Mail* 28 February 2000, A6.

34 Ibid.

35 Pugliese, David; "Strapped Forces face even more cuts," *The Ottawa Citizen*, 14 October 2000, A8.

Drivers of Military Spending

Military spending should be used for defending Canadian territory, legitimate defensive needs, or other specific roles such as U.N. peacekeeping operations.

However, there are myriad forces at play that work to push military spending beyond the specific purposes of self-defence. Globalization, the arms industry, and military allies such as the U.S. and NATO push for Canada to spend more on defence – much more than is required for our basic needs.

> *"...some experts suggest that Canada could never spend enough money on defence to make any significant military contribution to U.S. forces..."*

Too often, defence spending is used to achieve non-defence goals, such as subsidizing high-tech corporations, creating jobs in depressed regions, or promoting exports of military goods. Moreover, defence spending has been seen as a means of gaining greater international stature and influence, and of improving relations with Canada's largest trading partner, the United States.

The United States

In a remarkable admission on September 4th 2002, the U.S. Ambassador to Canada, Paul Cellucci, revealed that when he was appointed ambassador his only instruction from the Bush Administration was to work on increasing Canada's military spending. His comment prefaced further statements openly critical of Canada's military spending and calling for a larger and better equipped Canadian military.[36]

In the post-September 11th context, many pro-defence spending commentators have pointed to the quality of Canada's relationship with the United States as being related to the size and funding of Canada's armed forces. Many of these commentators have been equally critical of Canada's foreign policy and independent

---

36 Cheadle, Bruce; "Friendly advice: U.S. ambassador urges more military spending," *The Gazette (Montreal)*, 4 September 2002: A12.

Photo by Cpl Lou Penney.

initiatives such as the Landmines Treaty, the International Criminal Court, and other policies undertaken in an effort to assert "human security."

While some defence experts suggest that by boosting the military Canada will be given a warmer reception at the White House, the connection between Canada's military spending and relations with the United States is less than clear.

Canadian troops unloading from a U.S. C-17 transport plane. The defence lobby wants Canada to spend $2 billion to buy these planes from Boeing.

For example, some experts suggest that Canada could never spend enough money on defence to make any significant military contribution to U.S. forces that would warrant special attention from the White House.

Here again, David King of the U.S. National Defense University in Washington, D.C., is frank:

> "What might it take to make the Canadian Forces relevant to the U.S.? The short answer is defence expenditures in the realm of six per cent or more of GDP for a sustained period of 10-15 years before the U.S. would consider Canada a reliable military partner with a military of some noticeable, marginal utility."[37]

In other words: an impossible defence budget five times what it is today – or $60 billion a year.

Given the tremendous gap between the superiority of the U.S. military and the military capacity of its allies in NATO, including Canada, Canadians should question the motivation behind U.S. demands that Canada spend more tax dollars on the military.

A plausible reason is that as a major market for U.S. defence equipment exports, Canada is being expected to increase spending to buy more U.S.-built weaponry. During the Clinton Administration, U.S. policy placed arms exports at the centre of defence industry development in order to reduce weapons procurement costs and to keep production lines open for systems such as Lockheed Martin's F-16 fighter plane and other export-oriented weapons systems.

A 2002 U.S. Congressional Research Service report showed that the global economic downturn has reduced the size of the market for U.S. arms. U.S. global arms exports

---

37 King, David L.; "We need a Romanow Commission for Defence and Foreign Policy," *Policy Options*, April 2002 Vol. 23 No 03.

dropped from $19.4 billion in 1999 to $13.5 billion in 2000, dropping further to $9.7 billion in 2001, a decrease of 50 per cent in two years.[38] While still the world's largest arms exporter, the U.S. will continue to seek out new markets and expand existing markets such as Canada through additional military spending by its customers.

The United States' demands for greater military support and "interoperability" with its allies to fight the War on Terrorism translates into "Buy more military equipment from us." For example, Air Force Lt. Gen. Tome Walters, the director of the Pentagon agency that runs government-to-government arms sales, predicted the War on Terrorism would help with sales of U.S.-made warplanes: "The first question any nation should be asking is how do we link up as tightly as we can with American air power."[39]

Photo by Cpl Shawn M. Kent.

Three Canadian ships in a U.S. battlegroup near Afghanistan. New missiles on Canadian ships could be targetted and fired by the U.S. commander aboard the U.S. destroyer.

Defence Minister McCallum echoed this point in response to the U.S. Ambassador's "friendly advice" to increase Canadian military spending. "I confess, I was somewhat amazed to hear the pretences of the U.S. ambassador yesterday," McCallum told the House of Commons. "Now every ambassador, part of his job is to sell the products of his country. So I think part of his motivation there is, to a certain [degree, there are] U.S. large planes made by Boeing that he wants us to buy."[40]

However, while members of the defence lobby argue that additional equipment will make Canada more sovereign, in actual practice the opposite is true. The Department of National Defence is anxious to enhance its ability to fit seamlessly into the U.S. military so the Canadian Forces can join U.S. forces in wars around the world. Purchasing more sophisticated and powerful U.S. weapons will only allow the Canadian military to be placed under U.S. command easily, as was the case in Afghanistan.

Two recent arms purchases are noteworthy in this regard. DND is arming CF-18s with U.S.-made Paveway II laser-guided bombs. One thousand bomb kits have been ordered from Raytheon Corporation for a total cost of $17 million (U.S.), or about $27,000 each (Can.). In 1996 the Canadian Air Force spent more than $100 million on similar bombs for use against the former Yugoslavia. Defence analyst

---

38 Grimmett, Richard F.; *Conventional Arms Transfers to Developing Nations: 1994-2001*, Congressional Research Service, 2002.

39 Wolf, Jim; "Pentagon plays Afghan card to sell U.S. warplanes," *Reuters* 4 January 2002.

40 "Defence minister questions motives," *CBC Radio transcripts*, 12 October 2002.

> **"The fact that a U.S. commander can aim and pull the trigger of a Canadian missile aboard a Canadian ship is staggering..."**

Martin Shadwick noted that "the Air Force is keeping the ground attack capability credible with this purchase, but because of that they might start getting invitations to coalition operations that the government would rather avoid."[41]

Even more significantly, DND will purchase SM-2 surface-to-air missiles for its ships for $19 million (U.S.). The eventual cost of the program will be several times higher. Curiously, the SM-2 missiles are not fully functional when used with the radar systems on the Canadian patrol frigates. However, the missiles are fully functional when deployed on Canadian ships participating in a U.S. naval battle group using the advanced Aegis combat system. This radar and communications system used aboard U.S. destroyers is so sophisticated that when Canadian ships are deployed as part of a U.S. battle group, a U.S. commander can target and fire the Canadian missiles by remote control from his command ship.

The fact that a U.S. commander can aim and pull the trigger of a Canadian missile aboard a Canadian ship is staggering in its implications for Canadian sovereignty and defence policy. Considering Canada's only casualties in Afghanistan were at the hands of the U.S. military in a notorious "friendly fire" incident, military integration and interoperability with the U.S. military have become a distinct liability.

Ultimately, greater military spending does not increase Canadian sovereignty. While redirecting resources from social programs to expensive weapons, Canada will only become better suited for integration into U.S. command structures to fight distant wars. Moreover, Canada will never be able to make a significant military contribution to U.S. military power, as pointed out by David King of the U.S. National Defense University. But of even greater value to the U.S. is Canada's expression of political support through its military participation in the U.S.'s aggressive and increasingly unilateral campaigns.

NATO

NATO officials have frequently joined the United States in criticizing Canada for not increasing defence spending. NATO Secretary General Lord George Robertson used his first official visit to Canada in November 1999 to complain about Canadian military spending, despite the fact that Canada is the sixth highest military spender in actual dollars amongst NATO's nineteen members. Moreover, Canada spends three times more than the combined military spending of all seven Eastern European countries recently invited to join NATO.

However, NATO officials and Secretary General Robertson urge all members to increase defence spending (with the exception of the United States). At its 50th

---

41 Pugliese, David; "Canada wants fighters to pack more punch," *Defense News*, 26 August 2002: p.5.

anniversary celebrations in Washington, D.C., NATO launched an ambitious initiative to increase defence capabilities through an alliance-wide arms procurement strategy, called the Defence Capabilities Initiative (DCI).

> **"NATO is at best an unnecessary and expensive duplication of the U.N., and at worst a force thwarting the U.N. ..."**

To promote the Defence Capabilities Initiative, Secretary General Robertson berated NATO defence ministers for decreasing defence spending at the end of the Cold War. Lord Robertson complained that

> "The time for the peace dividend is over because there is no permanent peace – in Europe, or elsewhere. If NATO is to do its job of protecting future generations, we can no longer expect to have security on the cheap."[42]

The DCI program has been less than successful, but NATO continues to push for increased arms purchases by member states even when NATO expenditures already account for 62 per cent – nearly two-thirds – of the world's total military spending.

NATO has clearly been unable to adapt to the post-Cold War environment. Its continued reliance on a nuclear war-fighting strategy and the maintenance of vast arsenals of nuclear weapons of mass destruction underscores this point.

Some defence experts argue that NATO membership gives Canada an opportunity to positively influence the U.S. and other allies – however, it is equally the case that NATO allows the U.S. and other allies to negatively influence Canada in terms of nuclear policy and military spending.

Furthermore, Canadians remain committed to the United Nations and its approach to conflict resolution and peace-building measures. NATO is at best an unnecessary and expensive duplication of the U.N., and at worst a force thwarting the U.N. when it takes a position unfavourable to Western military interests.

The Global Economy

The architecture of the global economy reinforces defence spending as a means of maintaining industrially advanced, knowledge-based economies in those rich countries that can afford large defence budgets.

As discussed earlier, international free trade agreements place limitations on government intervention in the economy, be it through regulations, subsidies, state enterprises, or other programs designed to achieve domestic social or economic goals. However, security exceptions within all free trade agreements rescind these restrictive rules in areas the government defines as vital to national security interests. This means that governments are allowed a free hand in defence policy, military spending, and economic aid used to support the arms industry.

---

42 "NATO Secretary General calls for increased defence spending," *Defence Systems Daily*, 3 December 1999. http://military-research.com/story/page5974.htm.

Security exceptions drive government efforts to support Canadian industry through defence spending, instead of through other measures such as tariffs, domestic procurement of goods and services, and other tools that promote economic development. For example, Canada's most successful trade agreement which built its industrial capacity and created tens of thousands of jobs, the Canada-U.S. Auto Pact, was struck down by the World Trade Organization as a violation of its free trade agreements. The ruling resulted in the loss of thousands of Canadian jobs in the automotive sector.

Because the Auto Pact decision showed that industrial programs are clearly vulnerable to challenges through the WTO, Members of Parliament are now openly calling on the federal government to use military spending as a WTO-exempt means to create jobs in Canada. For example, the chair of the Standing Committee on National Defence and Veterans Affairs, Liberal MP David Pratt, wrote in *The Ottawa Citizen*:

> "The federal government's procurement of goods and services required for the purposes of defence, intelligence or security are not subject to international trade agreements signed by Canada. [...] At a time when many jobs have been lost in weakened high technology sectors, new investments in defence and security offer tremendous opportunities for Canadian workers, companies and technologies."[43]

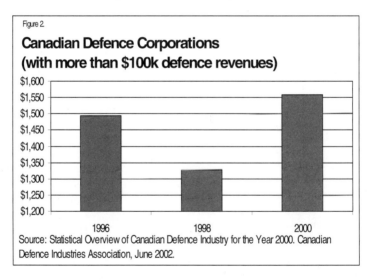

Figure 2.

Canadian Defence Corporations (with more than $100k defence revenues)

Source: Statistical Overview of Canadian Defence Industry for the Year 2000. Canadian Defence Industries Association, June 2002.

The pressure to help Canada's ailing aerospace and high-tech sectors with new defence contracts is intense. For example, Canada's national aerospace success story, Montreal-based Bombardier, is the third largest builder of civilian aircraft in the world. But its economic fortunes have been hit hard by the downturn in the industry since September 11th, leaving Bombardier to look for a government bail-

---

43 Pratt, David; "A new defence policy must fight for jobs," *The Ottawa Citizen* 8 December 2001.

out through military spending to restore investor confidence and maintain the federal government's influence in politically important Quebec.

Weapons Corporations

According to a June 2002 study by the Canadian Defence Industries Association (CDIA), Canada's domestic defence industry comprises 1,559 companies which

Table 4.
Defence Revenues by Market Segment 1996-2000 ($millions)

Market Segment	Defence Revenues ($millions)			% change 1998-2000
	1996	1998	2000	
Canadian defence market	$3,758	$3,211	$4,082	+22.6%
U.S. defence market	$996	$1,067	$1,254	+17.5%
Rest-of-the-world defence market	$798	$851	$1,494	+75.6%
Total defence revenues	$5,552	$5,128	$6,969	+35.9%

Source: Statistical Overview of Canadian Defence Industry for the Year 2000. Canadian Defence Industries Association, June 2002.

earned more than $100,000 in defence revenues in 2000.[44] Many of these companies are large aerospace and high-tech industrial corporations such as Bombardier, General Motors, CAE, and General Dynamics, among others.

Successive surveys of Canada's defence industry have shown an alarming increase in both the value of Canada's arms industry, and the number of corporations involved in military production. The defence industry generated $6.969 billion in military production and services in 2000. The latest report demonstrates how dependent the industry is upon Canadian military spending, as 59 per cent of defence revenue comes from within Canada. The remaining revenue is derived from exports to the United States and the rest of the world.

These figures are much higher than previously thought, and illustrate several worrisome trends. First, as the defence industry grows in value, this results in a significant sector of the economy becoming dependent on either Canadian arms expenditures or arms exports. The defence lobby's continuing push for higher levels of military spending will therefore be driven by industry's economic dependency.

The Organization for Economic Cooperation and Development (OECD), a think tank for the world's twenty-eight most industrialized countries, issued a warning

---

44 Statistical Overview of Canadian Defence Industry for the year 2000, Canadian Defence Industries Association, June 2002. Ottawa.

to its members that post-September 11th increases in military spending could damage their national economies. The OECD said in its report, *The Economic Consequences of Terrorism*:

> "One lasting impact [of September 11th] is the rise in defence spending in several countries since the attacks, which has reversed part of the post-Cold War period 'peace dividend'. Although increased military and security spending can give a short-term boost to the economy, it creates a longer-term risk of crowding out activity in other sectors."[45]

Second, to offset potential reductions in government defence spending or to encourage high-tech industrial growth, the government has become a business partner with arms manufacturers by assisting arms exports through financial, diplomatic and other means. This puts the government in the conflicting position of both regulating arms exports to ensure arms are not sold to repressive or conflict-ridden countries, while at the same time promoting arms exports.

Third, there is evidence that traditionally non-defence corporations will redirect their research and production towards military products and services in order to capitalize on increases in Canadian and U.S. defence spending.

Box 2.

Selected Canadian corporations with DND contract awards of $10 million or more (2000-2001)[47]

- Computing Devices Canada Ltd. (now General Dynamics Canada)
- Litton Systems Canada Ltd.
- Amex Corporation
- Atco Frontec
- Atlas van Lines
- BAE Systems Canada (now CMC Electronics)
- Bombardier
- CAE Inc.
- Compaq of Canada Limited
- H.H. Brown Shoe Co.
- IMP Group
- Irving Oil Limited
- MacDonald Dettwiler and Associates
- Oerlikon
- Raytheon Systems Canada
- Shell Canada Products ltd
- Thales Optroniques
- Victoria Shipyards
- Michelin Tires
- IBM

The CDIA study shows that the size of the Canadian defence industry is growing in terms of the number of corporations supplying military customers.[46] As well, the ranks of the top corporations receiving more than $10 million in contracts from DND include such unlikely corporations as Amex Corporation, Shell Canada Products Ltd., Compaq of Canada Ltd., Michelin Tires, and IBM, showing that the footprint of the defence industry is growing.

Fourth, the greater its reliance on defence spending, the more vulnerable Canadian industry becomes to the unpredictability of defence spending and arms programs.

---

45   The Economic Consequences of Terrorism, Organization for Economic Cooperation and Development, 6 July 2002, http://www.oecd.org/EN/document/0,,EN-document-0-nodirectorate-no-12-30611-0,00.html.

46   Statistical Overview of Canadian Defence Industry for the year 2000, Canadian Defence Industries Association, June 2002, Ottawa.

47   Ibid.

Canadian industry succeeded where U.S. industry suffered at the end of the Cold War because Canada's civilian-focused industries – especially the aerospace industry – were better prepared to adjust to reductions in defence spending.

A 1996 Industry Canada report on the aerospace industry said, "In countries such as the U.S. and France where, unlike Canada, a significant portion of output is bought by the domestic military, the end of the Cold War saw output and employment decline proportionately more than in Canada."[48]

Moreover, Industry Canada predicts that a focus on defence markets could be dangerous for the industry: "The ability to overcome the challenges and exploit the opportunities in the new global environment will vary by the nature of the activities in which the firm is engaged... Companies with a cost-plus military focus, dependent on military customers, are also vulnerable."[49]

---

48 Industry Canada, Sector Competitive Framework Series: Aircraft and Aircraft Parts - Highlights, 1996.
49 Ibid.

Choices for Canada

The Department of National Defence predicts a very bleak future for peace, human rights, and civil liberties in the wake of September 11th. Alarmingly, DND's "Strategic Assessment" says that foreign aid, international law, civil liberties, and even the lives of civilians will be casualties of the War on Terrorism, and there will be a "shoot first, ask questions later" approach to counter-terrorism.

> *"... in recent years Canada's influence has been derived from precisely the opposite of military power: our moral power."*

Its findings include the following:

"The balance between the notion of 'human security' and traditional concepts of security will likely shift away from championing poverty eradication and human rights.

"Previous concerns to...minimize collateral [that is, civilian] damage will be of less importance than achieving military objectives.

"Human rights/civil liberties may be circumscribed in order to provide enhanced security.

"The standards of proof for complicity for terrorist attacks before undertaking counter-terrorist actions will be relaxed in favour of results."[50]

All of these developments fly in the face of traditional Canadian support for human rights, foreign aid, and a respect for human life – even during times of conflict.

Given this assessment by DND, the federal government must resist these developments at all costs. Further bolstering Canada's military spending to increase its lethality and interoperability with the U.S. military as it embarks on President Bush's "war without end" is not in keeping with Canadian values.

Recent polls demonstrate that a year after the September 11th terrorist attacks, Canadians are becoming less inclined to desire close relations with the United States, are becoming increasingly frustrated with a variety of Canada-U.S. issues, and are opposed to Canada's participation in a U.S.-led war against Iraq.

---

50 Strategic Assessment 2001, Department of National Defence, Directorate of Strategic Analysis, September 2001, http://www.forces.ca/admpol/org/dg_plan/d_strat/strat_overview_2001_e.pdf.

> *"polling results clearly show Canadians do not want the country to follow the U.S.'s lead and invoke a military response to September 11th."*

According to a poll conducted by the Centre for Research and Information on Canada (CRIC), Canadian public opinion dramatically shifted away from desiring closer relations with the United States in the year following the terrorist attacks. In September 2002, 35 per cent wanted Canada-U.S. ties to be more distant – a dramatic increase of 22 points from a year earlier.[51]

Even more, four out of every five Canadians think that the U.S. bears some (69 per cent) or all (15 per cent) responsibility for terrorist attacks on them because of its policies and actions in the Middle East or other parts of the world.[52]

Canadians are viewing the previous foreign policy failings of the U.S., the terrorist attacks, and the military response and the ensuing War on Terrorism as a self-defeating cycle of violence. This is a cycle of violence that Canadians do not want to become embroiled in.

For example, a Leger Marketing poll taken in August 2002 found that most Canadians (54 per cent) thought that U.S. President Bush's arguments failed to provide enough justification for a war against Iraq, and that an even greater majority of people (57 per cent) were afraid that Canada's military participation in the war could result in reprisals from countries in conflict with the United States.

These results go far in explaining why a majority of Canadians (54 per cent) in September of 2002 told Ipsos-Reid that they do not approve of sending Canadian troops if the United States takes military action to overthrow Iraqi President Saddam Hussein.[53]

These polling results clearly show Canadians do not want the country to follow the U.S.'s lead and invoke a military response to September 11th. Instead Canadians want the federal government to provide leadership and take an independent position from that of the United States – especially in terms of defence and foreign policy.

Canadians want to play a positive role internationally.

The defence lobby has argued that an increase in Canada's military spending will allow the military to play a greater role in global affairs. In essence, they claim

---

51 "More Canadians distance themselves from U.S. neighbors," *Centre for Research and Information on Canada*, 9 September 2002, http://www.cric.ca/pdf/cric_poll/borderlines_ca_us/borderlines_press_neighbours_sept2002.pdf.

52 "84% Of Canadians Think That The U.S. Bears Some (69%) Or All (15%) Responsibility For Terrorist Attacks On Them Because Of Its Policies, Actions In Middle East, Other Parts Of World," *Ipsos-Reid/CTV/Globe and Mail*, 6 September 2002.

53 "Majority (54%) of Canadians Do Not Approve of Sending Canadian Troops If the United States Takes Military Action to Overthrow Iraq President Saddam Hussein," *Ipsos-Reid/CTV/Globe and Mail*, 4 September 2002.

there is a crucial link between Canada's military power and our international stature.

But as others have pointed out, in recent years Canada's influence has been derived from precisely the opposite of military power: our moral power. Columnist Lawrence Martin wrote recently in *The Globe and Mail* that our position as a non-nuclear middle power and our independent positions on Cuba, the Vietnam War, and even the Landmines Treaty, have given us much more influence than whatever military might we could afford would ever grant us. "American hawks scoff at Canada's do-gooder foreign policies on issues such as war with Iraq. But history has a habit of giving us the last laugh," he observed.[54]

Even worse, because Canada has been slowly moving toward a more U.S.-integrated foreign and defence policy and has focused much more attention on the "International Trade" side of the Department of Foreign Affairs and International Trade, our position in the world is slipping on more important peace and disarmament issues.

In fact, it wasn't Canada's level of military spending that made a mockery of Prime Minister Chrétien's initiative to exact greater economic aid for Africa at last summer's G-8 meeting – it was Canada's paltry foreign aid budget (which is about five times lower than its military budget). Moreover, developing countries are rightly distrustful of industrialized countries because of global free trade agreements that favour rich industrialized countries and corporate interests over the needs of poorer nations.

Once again, polling indicates that Canadians want the government to take a leadership role in helping Third World countries through aid and debt relief. A Leger Marketing poll taken last summer found that nearly half of Canadians (45 per cent) think the West doesn't do enough to help Third World countries, and that a third of Canadians (33 per cent) want an increase in Canadian financial assistance to developing countries.[55]

This generosity indicates that Canadians feel the War on Terrorism is not going to be won through military means. The same poll found that a majority of Canadians (56 per cent) feel that if richer countries increased their investments in poorer countries, it would have an impact on world peace.

Canadians feel security is derived from social programs.

Canadians are concerned about their security. But Canadians view security much differently from our American neighbours: Canadians tend to see security deriving from social programs, and playing a positive role in the world.

They are unconvinced by the defence lobby that the federal government should boost defence spending. A GPC Public Affairs and Communications poll released in October,

---

54 Martin, Lawrence; "History's on Canada's Side," *The Globe and Mail*, 10 August 2002: A15.
55 "How Canadians Feel about Third World Aid," *Canadian Press and Leger Marketing*, July 2002.

2002 found that "even after months of studies and newspaper stories about the state of the Canadian Forces, military spending has not gained ground as an area where Canadians think the government should increase spending."[56]

The defence lobby overlooks the fact that every dollar spent on defence means a dollar not spent on another program. These are the parameters within which the federal government develops the annual budget. Moreover, it has the obligation to respect the views of Canadians, not just experts and industry, when determining where tax dollars are spent. Public resources must be used for the greatest social benefit.

The difference in the economic and social benefits of investments in social programs is dramatic when measured against those of military programs. Military programs are very expensive, create fewer jobs than non-defence investments, and do not provide long-term benefits because weapons systems do not make contributions to the economy once built.

Table 5.
Spending choices: social programs vs. military programs.

Social program	Cost	Military program
Initiate a National Drug Program.	$500 million	Buy five new helicopters for the patrol frigates.
Build 20,000 new social housing units.	$2 billion	Buy six C-17 military transport planes.
Invest in public infrastructure such as water systems and public transit and create 60,000 jobs.	$4 billion	Buy military equipment and services and create only 22,000 jobs.
Implement Romanow Commission recommendation to restore federal share of health care funding to 25%.	$6 billion/year	Implement Commons Defence Committee recommendation to increase military spending by nearly 50%.

The respected Alternative Federal Budget produced annually by the Canadian Centre for Policy Alternatives and CHO!CES puts forward proposals to fund new social programs that are developed through a unique process that includes public input.[57] The proposals include real cost estimates and are compiled by a panel of economists to create a workable federal budget.

The results of successive budgets have shown that many social programs can be expanded and new programs created if the political will exists to redirect resources to those needs. Many social programs favoured by Canadians could have been in place years ago if resources had not been spent on big-ticket defence items. Decisions on future spending will determine whether resources will be available for a long-sought National Drug Program, social housing, and desperately needed improvements to health care.

---

56 Wells, Paul; "Military upgrade a low priority for most Canadians: Government should focus first on health care or environment, new poll suggests," *The National Post* 22 October 2002: A7.
57 "Alternative Federal Budget 2003 Economic and Fiscal Update," *Canadian Centre for Policy Alternatives*, 29 October 2002, http://www.policyalternatives.ca/afb/afb2003-fiscal-statement.pdf.

Conclusion

It is clear that the debate on defence policy and spending must be taken beyond Parliamentary committee rooms, university campuses, and newsrooms. For too long Canadians have been denied opportunities to participate in a discussion about Canadian military spending that has only included decision-makers and the defence lobby.

This report has assessed Canada's military spending from the perspective of its citizens – this means those people who live in Canada and in whose name these important decisions are made.

In the final assessment, Canada's military spending is already very high and has been growing alarmingly in the past few years. Canada's defence policy does not reflect the desires of Canadians, and is commanding too many fiscal resources in order to maintain ambitious, aggressive and outdated military capabilities.

Canada's defence policy should ensure that the country's legitimate territorial defence and sovereignty are met at the minimum cost necessary. In addition, the Canadians Forces should play a positive role internationally through non-combative U.N. peacekeeping.

By committing new resources now, the federal government would only be rewarding poor planning, mismanagement, and waste within the Department of National Defence instead of encouraging a rationalization of defence policy and better management practices by the military.

Furthermore, the federal government must ensure that policies for non-defence areas that affect defence, such as industry, trade, and international relations, do not become drivers of defence policy or defence spending. These policies must support a civilian-based economy that promotes sustainable development and human security.

Finally, the government should take steps to limit the ability of vested interests in defence to dominate the public debate on defence issues. The first step would be ensuring that citizens are provided with the necessary information and resources to educate themselves on defence issues independently of the Department of National Defence, and that civil society is included in the creation of both defence and foreign policies.